I'm not Shouting ©

By: Esther Litchfield-Fink

ISBN: 979-8-218-611863-6
Published by Litchfield Strategies, LLC
Florida, USA

www.estherfink.com

First edition
Printed in the United States of America

DEDICATION

*This book is dedicated to
my children, the light of my life.*

*Leah
Benny
Annie*

*And my animal
soulmates*

*Cookie (RIP)
& Oreo*

*& to all the women of the world, know this: You are
strong, graceful, & the art of this world, so love your-
selves unapologetically, fully and completely.*

Table of Contents

Me   *10*

1.	Hair	13
2.	Fearless Like the Homeless	17
3.	Anger is not Ladylike Said my Dad	25
4.	On Being a Rebel	31

Relationships   *36*

5.	He Wore a Cream-Colored Cardigan	39
6.	The Earrings That	
	Would get you to Like me	49
7.	When the Stoic Cries	51
8.	He Faded Away	57

9.   When he's Finally Gone   61

10.   We Never Made it to Your Birthday   67

Odds & Ends   *71*

11.   I Ate the Croissant I Bought for
my Kids   73

12.   On Crushing it   79

Random, Unimportant Thoughts   *86*

13.   What's Before Your Eyes   89

14.   It's Easy to Hope When
Things are Good   95

Happy, Funny and a Little Weird   *106*

15.   My Sock Has a Hole   109
16.   How to Solve a Rubik's Cube   117
17.   Dancing in my Room   125
18.   Dip Into Life   128

Music   *133*

19.   When I Hear the Bee Gees   135
20.   I Wish I Went to Woodstock   143
21.   Chappell Roan or God   149
22.   It's a Finneas Day   153
23.   He Played the Piano for me   158

Life's Questions   *160*

   24.   The Year of the Turning Tide   163
   25.   What Life do I Want   169
   26.   What Should I say, God?   173

Just Saad and Mad   *178*

   27.   Someone Say Something Nice to me   181
   28.   Don't Raise Your Voice   187
   29.   I Cry When Someone's Nice to me   191
   30.   Terrible News. I'm Not Sad   197
              Anymore
   31.   If God Reads Minds   203

Conclusion   *210*

   32.   With Apologies for Sad Poems   213

Me

Hair

i want her hair
if i had her hair
my life would be
perfect
well maybe not
perfect
but
close
her hair
is long
undone
waved around
by the wind
slept on
with a
non-silk
pillowcase
hair shaken
not stirred
untouched

i want her hair
the kind that says

i don't care
i'm living life
my way
no dye no style
no cut no color
no wig no weave
no thought
at all
the roll out of
bed
brush teeth
splash water on
face
and slip on
a clean
new
white t-shirt
and some of
yesterday's outfit
left on the chair

hair that you
know
can take you
far and wide

magnetizing
everyone and
everything
you didn't even
dream of.

what did she do to
her hair?
nothing.
it is how it is
like life

wake up
rinse out
wash off
shake
and
go
just
f*cking
go

fearless like the homeless

i watch the guy
walk
right along the beach
alone at 3 am
from the comfort of
my ocean view
room.

i watch the guy
walk
right along the beach
in the dark
and wonder
isn't he scared
to be out alone at
night?
he's not.

i watch the guy walk
right along the beach
fearlessly
while i watch
prepper TikTok's about the
coming
apocalypse
on my iPhone

listening to the
sound
of the
calmly slapping waves
that i paid a lot
to listen to
and see
for just a few
days
to calm me
down

but
i'm scared.

i wanna be
fearless
like that homeless guy
outside
he's not even
wearing a backpack
or carrying bags.
i mean i don't
leave the
house for five
minutes
without a backpack
and bags with things i might need
just in case

i watch the guy
walk
right along the
beach
as i feel
the cool air
coming from the vents
all around
the room
so it feels
perfect.

he must be feeling
the spray of the
ocean
now and then
and the inconsistent
breeze and the
sand between
his toes

i watch the guy
walk
right along the
beach
won't he be tired
in the morning?

it kind of is morning
at 3 am.

i leave the window ledge
i must get sleep
so i won't be tired
i paid a lot for this trip
to sit
in the
ocean-front room
and play all day
sun and sand

but wait
i don't want a day of sun
i don't want a day of play
i don't want a day of sand
with a password
to the gate
that leads me to the beach.

all i ever wanted
my entire life
even as a kid
was to be fearless
like the homeless man
walking the beach at night
with no backpack full of
snacks
no phone
and no maxed out
ATM card.

what will he do
for breakfast?
i doubt he's burdened
by that thought
while i wonder
about
the stack of pancakes
the cute cafe
on the corner serves
and how many hours
are left
until they open.

i watch the guy
walk
right along the beach
he looks slim
and trim
he succeeded
where i failed

all those hours at the
gym
and i still don't look
the part
of whatever i think
i came
to this world to play.

i now know what part
i'm here to play
it's the fearless part
like the homeless man
that walks on the beach
and watches the sun rise
and watches the sun set
fearlessly.
unburdened,
knowing the universe
will provide.

anger is not ladylike

'anger is not ladylike,'
said my dad

and we wanted to be
ladies
my sisters
my mother
and i
so we did what dad said
we kept it inside
all the while
he ruled the house
in a way
that
made us all
angry
and mom would
cry

'anger is not ladylike,'
said my dad
so we kept it
inside
and slowly
we forgot
that anger existed at all.

'show no emotions'

that was the rule
the way i was
schooled
you say certain things
like,

'thank you'
and 'please'

with a pleasant
demeanor
though he would be
meaner
but that didn't matter
to him

'anger is not ladylike,'
said my dad

so what did we do when
anger
peeked out
who am i kidding

anger doesn't peek
it rears an ugly
head
when kept
contained
drained
of being heard
for way too
long

funny thing is one
at a time
we each had
our way
to let it
come
out
mom would
cry
sometimes shout
and shut down no
communication or
conversation

sis would be
funny and loud
very dramatic

not follow the rules
at school
kicked out of class
and all would laugh
oh, silly sister!

and then there was me
i followed the
rules
no anger for me
i would just be perfect
and do what i'm told
not be bold
in walk
or talk
or dress
or stress
just toe the lines
drawn up by dad
and the
school.

smile and shine
be sublime
to and for
everyone.

anger?
what's that.
it didn't exist
until it did

cat's out of the bag
i decided one day
to walk away
to fly far away
to run on
beaches
paint pictures
write poems
have babies
leave unhealed men
have fun with healed
men

make money
go shopping
talk and talk
and talk some more

and never be
dad's kind of
ladylike
again.

on being a rebel

i'm rebelling
today
while you don't
you all could hold
the pin in the
grenade
keeping the world together
while i take a break
and let go
of control
of trying
to do the right
thing
or things
and more right
things.

i'm rebelling
today
while you don't
i mean
we can't all rebel together
and let loose
and play music
and dance
and eat at lunchtime
instead of starving
untill dinner.

someone has to
keep their
hands on the
wheel
ten and two
ten and two
adjust your
rear mirror
keep your eyes
ahead
and step on it
staying
within
the
speed limit
while i speed off

windows down
hair blowing
pretending i'm
thelma or louise
and just
killed
a man.

i'm rebelling
today
while you don't
i mean they
killed a man
but didn't they also
party with brad pitt
in the convenience store?
see,
when you rebel
you get the goods.

we were lied to
by
the ten and two people
minding the world
with all the right
cards
playing fair
and square
they never got
the joker.
jokes on them
apparently.

i'm rebelling
today
while you don't

i left the house
and like the good
gen-xer
i was taught to
be
i won't return
until it's dark outside.
ha ha the jokes on,
well, on me?
not to return home until
dark?

that sounds amazing
to a person
that hates dishes
cooking and laundry
and telling other people
to toe the line
be on time
stay inside
do what's right

i'm out and about
no laptop in sight
cruising the streets

and whatever grabs my
attention
i'm there
bag of snacks in the back
being a rebel in the night
till the lights come on
again

35

Relationships

he wore a cream colored cardigan

he wore a cream colored cardigan
the first time
we met
face to face
i mean
we met for
hours
on the phone
and text
we picked each other
out
from many
on a site
oh how random
(not random)

he wore a cream colored cardigan
i didn't know
he would
the first time we talked
his voice was
smooth
as wood
scented perfume

it wafted
in the
air
in my imagination
in my
bedroom
where i
half laid
leaning on my headboard
one leg
dangling
off
as if ready to
go
in case
he came knocking
at my door

he wore a cream colored cardigan
the first time
we met
i didn't know
what to
expect
from this
stranger on
tinder

who showed up
as living
in my
neighborhood
yet he didn't.
he lived
thousands of
miles
away
that should've been a
flag
of many
colors
ha ha
do you think
one sees flags
waving frantically
nope
those flags
wore the harry potter
invisibility
cloak

Esther Litchfield-Fink

he wore a cream colored cardigan
that did it
for me
you know that
moment
your fluttering
mind
makes decisions
for you
without asking?
well
alas it was happening
finally

all that talking
and passing
hours
upon
hours
of
electricity
what the heck
did we even talk about
ha ha who cares
who knows

it was heaven then
(pretend heaven?) maybe.
who knows
hindsight isn't better here
if anything, it's…
well never mind
does it matter now

meet me
at nine
a few weeks from
now
and miles
and miles
of conversation
well into the
night
and morning
were going to
collide

too much time
to wait
anticipate

but there
you have it
that's how it was
and one fine
cold
new jersey
nite
i showed up
at nine

and he pulled up
and stepped out of
his car
flowers in hand
fireworks
and so it was
the moment we met
the first thing
i saw
after his
smile
that lit up the night
ignited and scared
barely breathing
anticipating
there he was

he wore a cream colored cardigan
in the
dead of east coast winter
no coat
oh my god
that magical
sweater
had me at hello
one of those
'could've been bad'
that turned out to be
an evening
of everything
disney

for a time
it was fine
more than fine

yet
there's always a yet
a but
that bursts the bubble
bubbles always burst
at one point or another

it didn't happen
right away
it was months
down the line
you know how
when you blow
a bubble
and catch it
with the bubble
wand
and it
lasts for a while
teetering
on breaking

but you hang on
the bubble
obliges
for a bit
of magic

and then
it just
bursts
disappears
where do burst
bubbles go
i don't know

left with
reflections
on cardigans
and such
here's the thing
one thing
that a cream
colored cardigan
doesn't do:

it may make
you fine
as aged wine
cute-ish divine

but

it

doesn't

make

you

kind.

the earrings that would get you to like me

i found the earrings i bought
when you asked me out
they were the ones
JLo wore

she looked so
stunning
as she went about
her life
her men
her music

so, i thought,
"this is a shoe in,
you'll like me now!"

i found the earrings
i bought
when you asked me out
over the phone
as soon as we hung up
i ran to the mall
ok drove
above the speed limit
not caring
if i'd get in trouble
with the
law

i had an outfit to plan
a car to clean
shoes to buy
earrings to hang
to surround my face
like JLO
with long sparkling
flashy diamond-y
glistening
things
maybe if i sparkled
even though i'm
not the sparkly type i
could make it happen
and then
just then
you would say,

"Oh my god
look at those earrings,
i like you!"

and you would never
ever
ghost me
ever again.

when the stoic cries

the stoic doesn't
cry
i mean they're
stoic
that's what stoic
means - to not cry
no matter what
life comes out
with boxing gloves or
acid rain
bad news
or pain
disdain
of
friends
who want to do better
than them
but can't
or won't
they don't.
it's easier for friends
to put out the flame of
you,
the stoic.

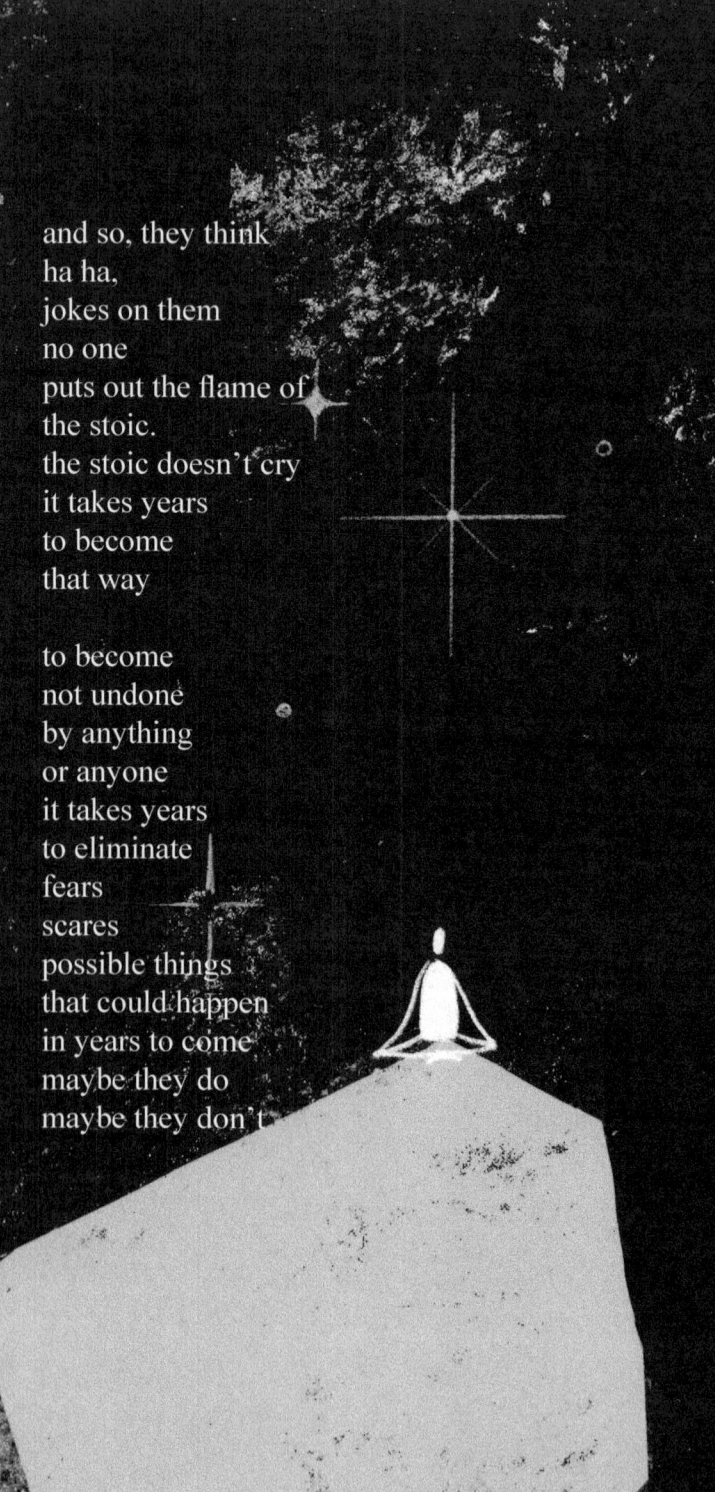

and so, they think
ha ha,
jokes on them
no one
puts out the flame of
the stoic.
the stoic doesn't cry
it takes years
to become
that way

to become
not undone
by anything
or anyone
it takes years
to eliminate
fears
scares
possible things
that could happen
in years to come
maybe they do
maybe they don't

well, some do
and some don't
but the stoic remains
well,
stoic.

the life of a stoic
is strong
tall
days are long
nights short
the stars
twinkle
and if they don't
the stoic still feels them
twinkling
because stoics see and feel
things
when no one else
does.

motionless
emotions in check
movements calculated
somewhat sedated mind
on purpose.

and yet
while the stoic
grounds
all the places
they go
and calms
the people they see
trees bow their boughs
flowers emit
scent
and birds whistle
silently
on tree branches
above the stoic
where they sit
and meditate
contemplate
the stoic
is proud.

until
one day
a sudden song
comes on
from the phone in
their hand
there was no
command

it just happened
plucked
by the tech gods
out of the
old playlist
they should have
deleted
but didn't

because I mean
they're stoic.
and it's the song
their song
i mean not anymore
and

so

the

stoic

cries.

Esther Litchfield-Fink

he faded away

you faded away
gray
just gray memories
i can see them in my mind
only if i squint

you faded away
gray
it took days
ok months.
fine, years, if i'm honest i
prayed hard.
i said, "GOD.
either give him to me
or take him
away, no in between."

but god didn't listen,

at least not right away he
left you there
sharp edges and all
i kept bumping in
and hurting myself
or was it you hurting me?
i don't even know.

and then one day
i didnt' say
one **fine** day
it wasn't fine.
just one day
you were faded away.

i realized
when i looked up
from the
book i was writing
from the
peace i was feeling inside
candle lit
on my desk
piano music in the background
another page
written.

i got up to refill my coffee cup
and when i sat back down
i had a hint
of a
memory
of you
drinking black coffee
with me,
one cold winter nite
laughing.

back to my writing
sipping my coffee
which now has milk and sugar
and it's warm in the room
i sit in a t-shirt
and let the memory
come and go
and fade into the background
of my life.

no sharp edges; no black coffee
just winds of time
blowing memories around
once in a while.

you see,
you faded away. it's OK.
i guess we're both happy this
way. if not
we don't know it too often.
that's ok
for gray to come and go
as long as the edges
that were sharp
wore down with time.
time does that - or is it god that
answered my prayers?
maybe that's it,
he slowly
faded you away.

Esther Litchfield-Fink ©

when he's finally gone

when he's finally gone
you're shocked
you stop
right in your tracks
those very tracks
you walked around in circles
waiting,
wanting,
worrying
to hear that you did nothing
wrong
to cause the great divide.

when he's finally gone
you're puzzled
befuddled
you expected to be
sucked
six feet under
with grief
and pain
shame and blame
a whip on your back
for not doing better
to keep the man
you (thought?) you loved.

when he's finally gone
you're not pacing
your heart's
not racing
you're suddenly facing -
what shall i call it?
peace.

for real?
can it be true?

no ice cream in dishes
no boxes of tissues
filled with devastating
sorrow
because you're waiting
for
tomorrow
he may text
or call
or not text
or not call
or god forbid
cancel plans again.

but wait. he won't do that.
he's gone.
it's the luck
of the f*cking draw.
his draw
because you could
always draw
whatever it would take
to make
your hearts
collide.

when he's finally gone
you find your days
a haze
of calm sunshine
seeping through the clouds
a breezy breeze
of
of
of
joy? laughter? lightness?

and so you put on the music
and dance
for the memories

for the past,
for the future,
and most of all
the
present.

you feel your fingertips
running through
your own
hair
you see your smile
in the
mirror
as you brush your teeth
you find yourself
dialing
new numbers
on your phone
to people you forgot about.

and he's finally
gone.

worry is gone
sorrow is gone
wishes are gone
plans are gone
waiting is gone
praying is gone
(sorry god)

but hope isn't gone
it's here,
in a new costume.
the costume is you.

you're back.

Esther Litchfield-Fink

66

we never made it to your birthday

we never made it to your birthday
not ever
and why do i care?

well
i found your birthday card
the one i got you
a long time ago
i'm talking years
before i knew
we would never make it
to your birthday

it has black leather
and a real zipper!
i mean i know!

we never made it to your birthday
not ever
why do i think of that today?
well
i was cleaning out
my closet
feeling all proud of
myself
for spring cleaning

and it wasn't even spring
and there it was
that birthday card
i forgot that i bought
at FAO Schwartz
there's an FAO
in JFK
who thinks of a
5th avenue toy store
in the airport?

but there it was!
Oh I love NY!

we never made it to your
birthday,
not ever
but when i milled around
FAO
and browsed the cards
while waiting for my
flight
i saw it
and i thought of you
i had to have it
you had to have it

it was that perfect card
you find
when you're not looking
so silly me
i bought the card
thinking
that 3 months away
i would mail it
and you would get it
and we would
laugh

but like i said
we never made it
to your birthday
not ever
i thought
that 'friends'
that texted
and sometimes chatted
would celebrate birthdays
together
in person, sometimes.

oh, silly me! as they say
the writing was on the wall
from the start

but hey who looks at walls
of writing
when you can instead
think of someone
that has this weird way
of matching their
heartbeat
to yours

from miles away
highways away
countries away
that should've had me
be able to tell
that if he's THERE
and not coming HERE
leave the birthday card
on the shelf for someone else
taking a plane
with time on their hands
that has no writing
on the wall

like i said, like i said,

we never made it
to your
birthday

Odds & Ends

i ate the croissant i bought for my kids

i ate the croissant
i bought for my kids
in the car
on the way home.
my intentions were good
don't they count?
when i was a kid
and got crappy gifts
i was told

"it's the thought
that counts"

so can i use
that gen x line
on gen z teens?
i think not
unless i want them to…
never mind.
there i go, using the
'dot dot dot'

i ate the croissant
i bought for my kids
i lasted
most of the way home

driving in
Miami traffic
and the closer i got
to home
to my kids
the louder
the croissant
called my name
and said,

"eat me"

i ate the croissant
i bought for my kids
on my way home
i planned on
taking one little
bite
but who am i
kidding?

no one.

i simply panicked
at the mere thought
of coming home
it's summer
vacation

and
i have a hard time
seeing people
on couches
relaxing
i keep forgetting
they study all year
and just got back
from camp

just seeing
a body on a couch
makes me want
to inhale croissants
over and over
until school
begins

i ate the croissant
i bought for my kids
i kept staring ahead
at the cars
and reaching in
and pulling off
bits
of the croissant

and then
i rolled up the bag
to save the rest
but then i remembered
it was chocolate filled
and i didn't yet
reach
the
chocolate

so i yanked it out
and one hand
on the steering wheel
and there it went
hoping the guy
in the next car
didn't see me
eating my way out
of noticing
anyone on couches
or enjoying
vacation

because there i was
putting myself
in a doughy
carb and sugar
coma

happy, relaxed
licking chocolate
off my fingertips
heading for a seat
on the
couch
as soon as i got
home

i mean it's
summer vacation
for all

on 'crushing it'

another 'crush your goals'
passed through my scroll
at 4:00 am today
i say don't
i certainly won't
crush anything
anymore

another 'crush your goals'
passed through my scroll
and i think of
my favorite people
in the world
did they crush goals?
they didn't.

my grandma
queen of grace
lipstick, perfume
and potato pancakes
she went to work
dressed up nice
came to see us often
but never once
did i see her
or feel like she was
crushing goals.

she listened to my stories
and told me hers
played songs
on the piano
brought chocolates
and did a lot of
sitting
on the couch.

i used to think
when i was small
that i would like to be
graceful
like her
when i grew up
and there was no inkling
of
goals or crushing.

another 'crush your goals'
passed through my scroll
and i think of
all
the goal crushing people
and how
when they talk of goals
and how they're crushing

their talk is fast
their walk is faster
their voice is pitched
their eyes are bulge-y-ish and
they show you
their transformed lives
and how you should and could
do it too

and if you don't
you're not part of
today
you'll be left out of
tomorrow.
i **so** want to be part of
today and tomorrow
but i don't want to
walk and talk fast
pitch my voice
bulge my eyes
and sleep less
so i can get those
early worms
they say are so
delicious.

another 'crush your goals'
passed through my scroll
and i hear the sound
of a bluebird
chirping outside my window
he's not crushing anything
he's just
singing.
i want to just sing too.

the scent of apple pie
comes through
my window
the lady next door
is up early
she's tasting and mixing
pouring and sifting
stopping to taste
what she bakes
flour
all over the place
and on her face
is a smile i'm sure
as she anticipates
the ones she loves
eating her creation
in elation
of a wonderful world
in the moment

while they wash
her apple pie
down
with lemon tea and honey
or steaming hot
coffee

i don't see any crushing
in that little story.

i saw on insta
there's a campfire
somewhere in the world
where all the 'crushing it' people
stand around
i don't think they have time to sit
they hold sticks
with big huge
fluffier-than-you-ever-had
marshmallows
and roast them in a
bigger fire
than anyone
as they share stories
of glory
and gory details

of how they got to be
at the
VIP crushing it campfire
of life

with cash in their pockets
crypto their kryptonite
heads spinning with
goals they will crush
because they must.

so maybe that's it!
some of us are made
to go around
rushing
and crushing
because that makes them happy
and know that they matter
so they chatter
about how we should do it to.

no thank you
i tried it
it's just not for me
you see i tried it
and failed to be happy that way.

i want to sing with the
birds while eating apple
pie

sleep until
my body says
it's ok to start the
day.

and most of all
have the time
to be kind
and really see
those around me
with attention
to the details of life
and be friends with myself
and that takes time.

and i can't do those things
if i'm crushing it.

Random Unimportant
Thoughts

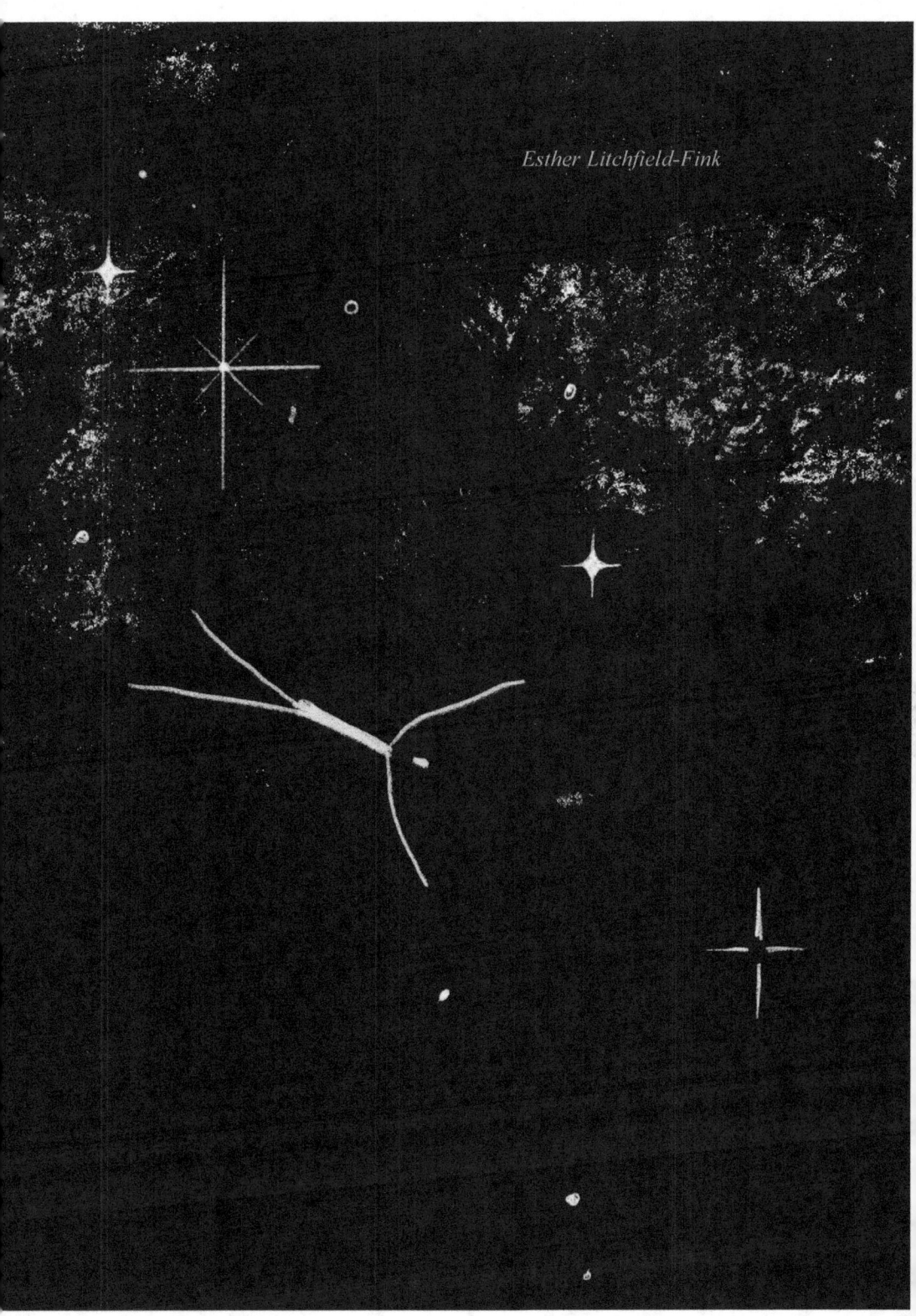

what's before your eyes

what's before your eyes
i ask
don't you see what's happening
oh silly me!
it doesn't matter
what's before their eyes
they see
what they wanna see
the fields are riddled
with truth bombs
all over the world

'but who wants
to see that?' they laugh

they look up
and see rainbows
they look left
and see stragglers
that didn't make it across
to the right side of the road
so they follow the authority

of
the
broken blinking winking
traffic light
they think is in charge of
their
destination.

what's before your eyes
i ask
don't you see
what's happening
the walls of the world
are closing in

"nah," they say
"silly you! walls can't
close! come, let's watch
the news over coffee
that will set us all
straight."

straight to where?
i wonder.
straight to
no one knows

the place that leads to
'oops that was not so good.'

ouch.

what's before your eyes
i ask
do you see what's happening
in the world
in the seas
in the storms
in the desperate pleas
of people
that try to warn us
then disappear

huh, that's weird
yet not everyone thinks so
and so it is

like the Dr. Seuss tale
of half the ducks
with stars on their bellies
and the other group
with none,
looking suspiciously
at one another

keeping their distance
which of the sneetches
are better?
rather, which is right?

to be stamped
with the star of wisdom
and insight brings fear
and calls to prepare
and those without the star
follow in line
step in time
march along
with a hum and a song
no care in the world

maybe that's what i'll do -
be a Dr Suess character
that sings
and rhymes
and dances
and hums
and has fun
while the titanic decides
if it's sinking

and maybe one day
we'll collectively see
that we don't actually see
eye to eye
because we are not supposed to
all see the same
be the same
live the same
and that's what makes
this wonderful world
go round
and round
and round

so enjoy the ride
whichever
sneetch
you
are

it's easy to hope

it's easy to hope
when things are good
'sublime!' we say
when asked how we are.

for the moment it's calm
there are no crying kids
tugging your
leg
no teacher complaining
no boss standing at your desk
demanding
you finish your work
while it's way past six
and your train left the station
at 5

it's easy to hope
when things are good
'hope and pray' we say
'it all works out
in the end!'

and it does!

as we pull up
and pump gas
without
having
to call the banker
for permission or hope
on a day that we know
we've got
way more than we need

we could feed
we could buy
we could fly
we could laugh
we could swim
we could play with our family
and friends
we have hope
for a better tomorrow for
everyone.

hope is all around
there are even hugs given and
kisses blown
in the wind

it's easy to hope
when things are good
what happens
when
through fate
or mistakes
or on purpose
through fault of your own
the problems arise
you stub your toe
as you get out
of bed
and the snowball begins
to roll
downhill

you step on the scale
don't like what you see
pink slip in your email
war conversation
in your tiktok feed
no longer filled with
happy dancers
now it's soldiers
in countries
you never visited
sons of mothers
someone's brother

will they come back home?
where's the hope now

it's easy to hope
when things are good
until they're
not
you don't get that text back
you're blocked
or maybe
you're the block-er
maybe your man
slammed the door
on his way out
or she packed you snails
for lunch. again.

hope is gone

with the toe
you can never un-stub
with life that is hard
the tests
that we get
from the universe
wrestles our hope
out of our hands

fear sets in
how will we even
survive
with the things
we go through
or see others go through

it's easy to hope
when things are good
when our hands are tied
our hearts are heavy
our legs
don't want to
touch the ground
in the morning
we don't like what we see
what we feel
for us
for others
suddenly it's that 'house
of cards' we see
falling down all around.

so you take out
the biggest shovel
you have
and shovel
the piles of snow
coming down

and when you stop
you turn around
and
it's still piling up
all over again
no matter what you do

you look up to the sky
shout 'WHY'
and keep shoveling
furiously
until you drop
to your knees
and remember
that that's the way to
pray

and so you stay
on your knees
for a moment
and
finally let go

you're simply too tired
to even get up
from down
on the ground

you can see the roots
of the trees,
the earth
the beginning of things
you have time to look
around and notice
that all of life begins again
from down
on the ground
and your silence and breath
joins the flow
of life
as it is

the snow falls all around
and without a sound
you stand up
and look around and see
there is still beauty
and possibility
as the snow keeps falling.

you don't know what will
be
if it will stop
or when

but then
your mind
quiets down
your heart opens up
and leads the way
and hope comes
from this new place
from the broken heart
not the head
and you're led
and know
there is always hope
for everyone
for everything

snow will always fall
yet it will stop
and give you a chance
to breathe
and hope
from
that place of certainty

and when it starts
again it's back
to
knees on the ground

and your heart's open
wide
that's where
you'll find
exactly what
you've been looking for

it may take time
but in a while
what you're looking for
will find you
right
where
you
are

Happy, Funny and a Little Weird

my sock has a hole

my sock has a hole
but i'm happy today
what do people do
with holey socks
pray for money
to buy new ones,
i guess.

but i kinda
like keeping that
as my secret
something no one
knows
it's inside my addidas
so on the outside
i look all put together
but i'm
unraveling

my sock has a hole but
i'm happy
i didn't say
i was happy yesterday
or even ten minutes
ago

but i just
got on the scale
and it was way down
all because
i forgot to eat
yesterday
because i saw the hole
in that sock
and felt like
the biggest
loser on planet earth

i'm attached to those
favorite socks
with the little RL logo
that pretends
i'm in
with the in crowd
that club
i really want
no part of
and there was the hole

i discarded
so many things
this year
i just want to
hang on
to something
for dear life

so if it's wearing
my favorite socks
that make me feel
complete
then so be it

but that unraveled
with that hole in the
heel
aren't holes in socks
usually
at the toe part?

i can't even
unravel
correctly.

my sock has a hole
but i'm happy
the sock is on
i'm dressed
and ready to go
what a weird
world

one minute i'm in bed
like lead

my head
glued to the pillow
hating mondays
and then
coffee calls
my name
and seduces me to
wake up
and smell the
roses

and that
snowballs into the
stumble
to get dressed
the fumble
for the
scale
the number
that i like
and the socks
that comfort me
hole
or
no hole

and i am off
in a whirlwind
of emotions
i'm taking the day
off
to go down
to the beach
and talk
to the water
and hear
what it has to say

and it will be
a lovely
lovely
holy
day

how to solve a Rubik's cube

i can solve a Rubik's cube
i'm not bragging
i was forced
coerced
so now i feel like a
genius

but ha ha the joke's on me
anyone can do it
if they follow
a set of rules
only i'm not a good rule
follower
anymore
so hey it IS a big deal

i can solve a Rubik's cube
i'm not bragging
my son forced me
to learn
he taught me
every morning
he handed me a cube
as i was juggling breakfast

packing lunches
and snacks
and aiming for
a calm morning
and in the midst
of this
he wants me to
be a genius.

i can solve a Rubik's cube
i'm not bragging
it took weeks
i'm embarrassed to say
i did not want to learn
ever
but this teen kept insisting
maybe
he wanted a mother
that has control of life
a mom that can rise
to the top of something

he asked me
why i'm not a millionaire
and i said because
i always only wanted to be
a writer
and i succeeded

so
i forgot to want things like
being a millionaire
maybe i should've
but it never entered my mind
his response was
to teach me to
solve the
cube.

maybe it's like any kid
that wants their parent
to be different than they were
like i wanted my
mother
to be like my
friends mothers
and remember things
like being on time
to pick me up from school
on sunday
when there was no bus
service
so i wasn't the last
one waiting
and waiting and waiting

or like wanting my father
to have been

a regular dad
not one that served
in the navy
and ran our house
like it was the military
but to be, you know,
just regular.

i can solve a Rubik's cube
i'm not bragging
my kid taught me fiercely
he did not let up
he did not want
a dumb non-millionaire
mother
that can't solve the cube
even though kids can do it
but that's what he got

so at the very
least
he wanted me to
solve
the cube
so maybe he could be
proud?

do i do that to him,
i wonder
want him to be
what he's not?

maybe this is his
revenge
for me dragging him
to friday nite
dinners
so he will be social
in our new neighborhood
but maybe he
doesn't want to be
social
and eat chicken that's not nuggets
at a neighbor
minding his manners
in a pressed long sleeve
white starched shirt
and listen to cringe adult conversations.

i can solve a Rubik's cube
i actually AM bragging
it was so goddamn hard
for me

i know 5 year olds do it but
my brain
is stuck
on
my kid wanting me to have
a million dollars
and how to let go
of my military dad
who's long gone
and isn't going to change
and how to get out of
the dinner i said yes to
for next friday night
and the times i told
this kid
to change his t-shirt
even though he was happy
with the one he was wearing
but i wanted a different look
for him

so the Rubik's cube is
solved
i hope he is proud
i actually think he is
and i'm exhausted
from all that thinking
and various algorithms

and wanting to
throw it in the lake
and also wanting to
make him proud
of having a mother
the type he really
wants
and if a Rubik's cube
could bandaid
the millions i didn't chase
because i was after my
name in print - then so be
it
i wear the
CUBE BADGE of honor
if there is one

now i mentally write up
a contract
with my kid
my mom
my dad

to each of us letting
each other
be who they want to be
do what they want to
do

wear what they want
to wear
eat dinner
where and what they want
not solve cubes
they don't want to solve

and we will
all
salute
the genius
of the
cube.

dancing in my room

no one sees me
dancing in my room
i mean who wants to see
a pretend Rockette
with a headset
and some rock 'n roll
music blaring
in her ears
and she dances
like she just won't care
what anyone says
about her moves

no one sees me
dancing
in my room
up on the bed
strumming my fake guitar
in the air
like i don't care
about a thing.

that would not look good
on my resume.

no one sees me
dancing
as i brush my teeth
winking at the mirror
as i bust a new move
and groove
thinking i'm back in the day
when it was ok
to show the world
you're happy to play
at the start of your day
at 4 am when no ones watching.

no one sees me
dancing
but they see me
working
and thinking
and doing
and going about the world

keeping the pieces together
as if it makes a difference.
no one sees me
dancing
when the world is still asleep

that's when i wake up
and think,

'it's gonna be a great day!'

and i forget
that only i can hear the music
coming from my headset
that the world is still deep asleep
and most wake with dread
at what's ahead
for them to shuffle through
and do, and do and do.

no one sees me dancing
maybe they should
then they would
join me in joy, heartbeats and more
as we crank up the sound
jump on the couches
spin 'round the tables
laugh in the mirror
grab some hairbrushes
sing to each other
and forget
that we get to be happy
as we choose

what's there to lose?
only sadness.

dip into life

dip into life
and life dips back
like bowing
and curtsying
to the king or queen
as you pass by.

when life shows you joy
or beauty
or just plain
luck
you throw back your head
laugh
call a friend
cry out,

"you won't believe
what i met with today,
it was serendipity herself!"

dip into life
and life
dips back
an encounter on a plane
a meeting in a
park

a flower at your feet
that you
step over
turn around
and pluck
and put in your hair
or lapel
and its scent
gives you pleasure
all day
discovering a connection
where it
wasn't expected

woosh!

serendipity herself
reveals
the magic
present in the world
sometimes

she has a rule:

you must dip
for life to
dip back

when you have a scowl
on your face
your nose
to the ground
a grunt
and a groan
about the truth
of life
that it's hard
it's
really hard

just know
that
no-one's to blame
for not dipping into joy
tall grass
and musical songs
and dances
but if you want
to be visited
by
miss serendipity herself

she requires it

so dip into life
and life will
dip back
don't hide
don't shut the
shades
and say you're tired
even though you are
or you could miss it

those moments
when miss serendipity
pokes her head out
from the tall grasses
in the fields
from the malls and the
halls
the schools
and the cities
the countries
all over the world
and wants to dance
with you
and
sprinkle magic dust
of a little luck
on you
and your life

so keep your hearts open
your head up
chin up
eyes open
hands free
to welcome
those moments
few and far between
that change your life
forever

Music

when i hear the bee gees

when i hear the bee gees
at 4 am
when i can't sleep
it makes me wonder
why people fight

barry and his brothers sing
that "nobody gets
too much love
anymore"
and that was years
and years
ago

when i hear the bee gees
at 4 am
i wonder about how
there must have been
fighting
way back then too
when they wrote that song
and now there's fighting
here too
but why were they fighting
then?

all the while
the bee gees were singing
about
men and women
in and out of love
like waves
or passing
cotton candy
clouds

when i hear the bee gees
at 4 am
i wonder if they knew then
that the little
squabbles
between men
and the women they love
would turn into
well
this
what's going on today
i can't even say it
i don't think they knew
what the world
would
become

when i hear the bee gees
at 4 am
i don't wonder anymore
about how they sang,

"if nobody gets
too much love anymore
it's as wide as a river
and harder
to find."

that's true.

"nobody gets too much
heaven no more…"

but why?

the bee gees knew it then
way back then
now the songs
are different
they are far from love
and are now saying,

"give me one good
prayer, i'm hanging by a
thread

one good prayer that
will open
the gates
of heaven."

we're so desperate.

maybe their songs
are a prayer
a call for
love
between one and
another
the songs today
they're a cry
for prayer
for peace
no mention of love

who can even think
about love
when you have to
beg with prayer
we're begging
no space for loving?

has anyone told the
bee gees
what happened to
songs

since they sang
that nobody
gets
too much love anymore?

i'm not going to
be the one
to tell them
and spoil it
and spoil their song
about wanting
just a little
bit
of love

when now
who can think of
love
when we first
need peace?

when i hear the bee gees
at 4 am
they draw me in
to their song
and
i think -

well maybe once again
love can come
before peace
and
before prayers are
answered
while hanging
by a
thread.

all of us
collectively
maybe we can say
one,
two,
three,
go
and let go
of lack of love,
the fighting,
and just listen
to the bee gees
sing about love
believe
in
love

and there will be no more
war

only peace
and love
for whoever stopped,
took a deep breath
and is listening
to the
music
of the
bee gees.

i wish i went to Woodstock

i wish i went to woodstock
but it was before my time
do you know
where i'd be today
if woodstock happened
in my day?
certainly not
talking to you

i wish i went to woodstock
for a few days
i would have been
in a daze, a haze
of music
no one calling out -
can you turn
the music down
stop playing that same
song
on the piano
stop humming
and strumming

there's work to do
things to get done
you'll have fun
later

we all know
how that ends
that road doesn't
lead to
woodstock

i wish i went to
woodstock
i would have never
come home
to the drone
of small town existence
where rules
replaced notes
on the sheets of music
in the air
in the mud
in the trees
in the hearts
in the souls
in the joy
in the laughs
in the love

of those that knew
there was a world
outside
of to do's and
to don't-s
don't go
don't stay
don't play
don't laugh too loud
or shout
or curse
just hurt in silence
and
go with the flow
that doesn't
flow at all

i wish i went to
woodstock
but i sure didn't
so i'll go now
and get some
bell bottom things
and grow my hair
long
and turn up a song
and close my eyes
turn my face to the
sky

and pretend
for a moment in time
that i could turn back
the clock
and take the road
less traveled
to woodstock

and what it'd be like
to listen
to
songs
all day long
i'd write poems
and dream
i'd be in San Francisco
for sure
thinking back
and wondering
what life would be like
if i had gone home
to my small town
after
woodstock

chappell roan or god

chappell roan or god
do i have to choose
can't it be both?
nope
when chappell comes on
i think back to the days
when hippies
had freedom
and rebels
would sing,

'go your own way'

and the gold dust woman
would go
her own
way
i wanna be a
gold dust woman

chappell roan or god
do i have to choose
can't it be both

i have a feeling
god is puzzled
by the
musical moan of roan
she sounds like -
oh never mind

when i was a teen
and madonna
was y'know
for the very first time
and i didn't know why
they shut the radio
and stuck record players
in front of us
with little
church boy choirs screeching
i mean singing
about godly things
the magical music
was kept out of earshot
and not to sound old
but back in the olden days
they controlled what we
heard
said
ate

they controlled
where we went
what we had
what we didn't have
what we did
what we didn't do

all they needed
to keep the chappell roan's
away from us
was a whip and a threat of god
funny how times have changed

well not that much
the roans of the world
do the same -
use god and whips
the un-threat of god
and the whip, well,
as they choose
there you go
what's old is new
what's new is old
and at the end of the day
it's all
about my one true and first
love, the music.

it's a finneas day

it's a finneas day
if you know, you know
if you don't
scroll on
it all started
in bed
the bed i didn't
want to get out of
those are horrible beds
that push you out
into the world
of ringing alarm clocks
that boss you
around.

it's a finneas day
if you know, you know
if you don't
scroll on

oh, you, you're still here
reading
and you don't even know
who finneas is

i can see you.
go away,
you're not magical
and musical
see that's a hint
of the kind of day it is
for me anyway

it's a finneas day
if you know, you know
if you don't
scroll on
it's only 7 am
and i bit my lip
while chewing gum
i spilled my coffee
all over
my favorite
white sneakers
that are 4 years old
maybe those
have got to go

and perhaps
i don't need caffeine
in my bloodstream
on a finneas
day

people around me
will be better off
if i have
a tall drink of water

it's a finneas day
if you know, you know
if you don't
scroll on
maybe i could blame
he boring date i had
this week
at a nice restaurant
with tasty meats and drinks
what could be worse
then a boring date?
the world
is so vast and interesting
if you're boring me
do you live in a hole or
something?

ugh he wasted my time
i need something
to cheer me up
the thought of that
makes me dig my heels in
deeper

it's a finneas day
if you know, you know
if you don't scroll on
how does one change
a finneas day
into a pharell 'cause i'm happy'
day
or a Queen
'we will rock you go-for-it get-
it-done
you-can-do-it
you're-the-best
kind of day?'

nah, once you're in
a swampy glorious mess of
finneas
you're not sneaking
your way out
with
freddie mercury.

'stay put'
i tell myself.
'stay put' and wallow.

and so i sit in my
car and wallow.

and what do you know
the sun began to
blind my eyes
and warm
my face.
i felt an inch
better

i turn on the music
and it's
finneas!
what do you know
he's singing about
breaking his heart
again.
aw, i wanna
tell him not to be sad
there are always
more hearts
like city buses,
they come and go

but if he goes outside
there's always
the
sun.

he played the piano for me

he played the piano
for me
one night
my ear
pressed
to
the phone
while he
sang
billy joel

he played the piano
for me
one night

the end.

159

Life's Questions

161

the year of the turning tide

the tide comes in
the tide rolls out
another year
goes by
and there's not
a single thing
i could do about it.

hey, who said
i gave anyone or anything
permission
to make me a year
older?
ahh birthdays they call it

'hold up, tide, stop
i said stop!'

but there's only
soft laughter
as the lapping waves
high five each other and
say,

'she made it!'

the tide comes in
the tide rolls out
leaving
seashells
full of little pearls
of wisdom
and fun
scattered on the shore
bathing
in the sun
ready to be strung together
for a new year
a new age
yet unknown
a gift
wrapped up
waiting to be
opened.

the tide comes in
the tide rolls out
leaving behind
in the ocean
of life
whatever was,
whoever was,
whoever wasn't.

the year has passed
no different than the sun
guaranteed to set
guaranteed to rise
hiding behind
the clouds sometimes
yet we know
it's
there.

the tide comes in
the tide rolls out
fluid
this early morning

there are 22 hours left
to celebrate
and contemplate
that all those years ago
on the 28th of February
one minute i wasn't
then the next
i was
born.

so here i am
still standing somehow

by the grace
of, well, everything
and everyone
that shared spots
on the journey with me
so far

the tide comes in
the tide rolls out
plans
for what's ahead
are milling around
on pause right now
while i'm taking it in
all that has been
and letting roll out
all that will be coming
for me

created, manifested
bringing in
sending out
my wish list
to the universe

'bring it on
bring it on!'

i say this
as if one could
even stop the tide

i laugh at my joke!

and laugh and
laugh some more.

the best way
to usher in
a
birthday

what life do i want

what life do i want
certainly not mine
i mean i'm laying around
at 10:06 pm
listening to camilla
sing about havana
but she's in LA

what life do i want
whatever i choose,
it better include bread
i'm sick of my bread-less life
i mean i'm so hungry for bread
i forgot
why i stopped having it
in the first place

what life do i want
the perfect one of course
like i see on instagram
i mean i know blah blah blah
it's not real
it's just perfect for a second
so we could all
eat our hearts out
and drool.

what life do i want
the one that comes with
a big pink eraser
the one i had in grade school
where i could quickly
erase
over any mistake
before the teacher reached
my desk.

i could use that
right about now
i made a few mistakes
that look bad on my test
of
life
mrs. nyman would say
i'm failing
no she would say i was a
failure
there's a difference.
and we all knew
she was the
holy
authority
on failure.

what life do i want
i stand up and look
in the mirror
blood rushes to my head
i apply some
lip gloss
and notice
how slim i look ohhlala
i'm liking
what i
see

i reach for my tripod
and mount my camera
and snippity snap
what do you know
i'm up on the gram
looking glam
like those whose life
i want to
live
so now others
will be stopping
their
insta scroll
when
my pic passes by

and they'll eat
their hearts out
instead of bread
because now
THEY can't eat bread
so they'll look like me!

so now that someone else
is eating
hearts
i can go back
and put on my ratty old
t-shirt
and eat bread
in bed
and listen to
camilla

oh camilla
who cares where she is
i'm happy
and
don't want anyones life
other than my own
bread
eating
one
in pajamas.

what should i say God

i'm all mixed up
one school of thought
says to relax
things happen for a reason
just as they
should.

be present
acceptance
surrender
breathe

so i'm breathing and relaxing
nothing's happening
i mean the breathing thing
is keeping
me
alive

what should i say
god
i'm all mixed up
others say to
hustle
and grind
if you wanna shine

don't just sit there
the early bird
gets the
worm
so go ahead -
demand
your wishes from the world

and so i stamp my
demanding foot
and now
i killed a bug crawling by
just at that demanding
stamping moment
poor thing

i saw the dead bug and forgot
what i even
wanted

what should i say god
i'm all mixed up
is it luck
or something else
is it all pre-planned
and the joke's on
us?

we're milling around
trying to find the right way.
thinking
we
make things happen,
heads held high
when we're outside
so everyone
thinks
we've got it together
and know
just what we're doing

but when we go into our
screened in porches
shoulders slouched, head down
contemplative
furrowed brow
to meditate
think and pray
in a bit
of disarray
and the stray mosquito
that got in
comes to land on our hand

so now i'm sitting
and meditating,
manifesting and praying
and scratching
until i draw blood
and my concentration
is
gone

i reach for the box of
band-aids
they're elmo band-aids
and i stick one on
i mean now it's
funny
at least i'm laughing
at the fact
that elmo's smile
staring up at me
is huge, white,
and disproportionate
to the rest of his
body
and he doesn't seem to care
and no one else
seems to
mind

so here's what i'll say god
guess what
i'm not mixed up
we're supposed to do it ALL
hustle, grind, cry, pray, stamp
meditate
and keep mosquitoes out

and when they get in
do something
to cheer up and smile
so at the end of the day
when your head rests
on the pillow
and you have a smile
on your face
that's disproportionate
with your life
that's how it was created to be

don't worry - be happy
however you get
to the porch of your life
at the end of the day
you did it

and that will have to be
the right way.

Just Sad and Mad

someone say something nice to me

someone say something
nice to me
is that so hard
ok you sometimes do
once in a while
and that's fine
i survive well, thank you
with my own
affirmations
and pats on the back i get
when leaning
up against
the grand old willow tree
in my backyard
overlooking a lake
where i lean
when it's a bit windy
and the branches sway
and
pat me on my back
and even a little on my face
and arms
and legs
as the rays of sunshine
acknowledge me

someone say something
nice to me
don't tell me to love myself
in front of the mirror
in my bathroom
at 4 am
as i get ready
to grind out my
day

here's a little secret
i don't 4 am anymore
i don't grind anymore
those days disappeared
locked outside my door
during lock-down
i also forgot other things
outside
with the lock-down lockouts
like
rushing
grinding
unkind people
criticism
work faster demands.
oh, that doesn't work
anymore

someone say something
nice to me
i'm leaving
the gen-x hard work ethic
in the dust
as i happily follow the lead
of the gen-z-ers
called 'quiet quitting'

i don't know what exactly that is
but i'm doing it
i'm quiet quitting
it sounds quite nice

GOGGINS shut up for once
you've been in my head for 3 years
and served me well
i followed you everywhere
rather you followed me in my brain
i'm putting you out
with the lock-down lockouts
even though they're over

why you ask?
because i sat down for a moment
while i was quiet quitting
waiting for someone
to say something nice

and that wasn't happening
do you know what happened
as soon as i sat down?
i felt God pat me on the back
and whisper,

"good job, you learned your
co-vid lesson
and now you are still
and can hear me,
that's what it was all about
anyway for you,
so pay no heed to criticizers
or put downers
you passed the test
better than the rest
i will sit here with you
on your stoop
and revel in the joy
and peace
of knowing
that it's all ok"

if no one has anything
nice to say
didn't their mothers
teach them

that if you don't have
something nice to say
to not say anything?

oh, so we're blaming mothers again
for the ills of society?
let's not do that
anymore
throw that out on the stoop
slam the door shut
leave it out with the lock-downs
and come sit
with a hot cup of cocoa
and
scroll through
funny tik-toks
pat ourselves on the back
laugh
and wink at ourselves
in the mirror
take a deep breath
and remember how fleeting
this all really is.

memento mori,
people.
memento
mori.

don't raise your voice

don't raise your voice
my father would say
but he would raise his.
in the world of the man
the plan
was to keep us silent
smiling
while we followed the rules
his rules

don't raise your voice
my father would say
but he would raise his.
and so it was
do as i say
not as i do

don't raise your voice
my father would say
but he would raise his.
to keep us in line
the line he set
the be met
without question

don't raise your voice
my father would say
but he would raise his.
so i learned to use
my outside voice
inside me
on my mind, that denied
on my heart, that cried
on my soul, that yearned
to be heard
and my stomach
turned
with all the unspoken
with all the un-shouted
with all the silenced
with all the sounds
shut down
to the ground
that humans
need to make
or
they shake
and quake
with fear
of the world

don't raise your voice
my father would say
but he would raise his.
until one day
all the un-raised voices
of all the world
found each other
and
joined together
and staged a revolution
to find a solution
for a place and space
to award
the un-raised voices
their time
in the sun

and once set free
the un-raised voices
spread
like dandelion fluff
blown once
with closed eyes
and the seeds got planted
everywhere
never to be contained again.

and so
voices will be raised
whenever
wherever
however
forever
never to be
silenced
again

as long as dandelions shall live.

i cry when someone's nice to me

i cry when someone's
nice to me
i thought i was healed
apparently not
Maya Angelou said,
she had so many
rainbows in her
clouds.

i had so many
clouds
don't know about the rainbows.
am i colorblind
what rainbows?
where are the rainbows?

i squint and look up
and down
and all around
gray
i see gray
yet i'm a-ok

i cry when someone's
nice to me
i work out in the gym
run on the track
strengthen my mind
to keep out
attacks
from the muggles and judges
the simpletons of spirit
roaming the earth
thinking they can judge
because they first say,

'no offense'

before they offend,
turn up their noses
and look down
the self-appointed
kings and queens
criticism, they say,
constructive.

i mean they could be family,
friends, teachers and neighbors,
plumbers
and appointed
community
helpers

they come along
when you have a
'stub your toe
in the morning'
situation
leading to
the tear in your stocking
on the way to start your day
the bump
and the thump
you hear from your front
right tire

you're tired
and the snowball
effect is in full damn force

i cry when someone's
nice to me
in the middle of a
snowball life
where things
are heading at you
full force
nonstop

and along the way
come the muggles and clouds,

'tsk tsk, you did wrong again'

they're helping the old lady
across the street today
but tomorrow,

'you're on your own, lady -
get it the f*ck together
what's wrong with you,
we helped you
yesterday
out of the goodness of our
excellent, perfectly orderly-
life hearts.'

and so i have developed
a mind of steel
and no one can offend
or criticize
hurt or penalize
judge
or say anything to me
that makes me cry
or feel bad or sad
i'm strong, i've got this life
together!

i take care of me
even laugh and play
like i said, i'm a-ok

so don't you dare
be nice to me
cz that makes me
suddenly
feel
my heart

and then i cry
and cry

and

cry

terrible news i'm not sad anymore

terrible news
i'm not sad anymore
do you know what that means?
the world
will now miss out
on the words
of my bleeding heart
and broken soul;
the devastation that comes
from being sad
and mad
at the events of life
i've been thrown into

i poured my words
mercilessly
and generously
out for you
and now what, what now?

terrible news
i'm not sad anymore
i was afraid
this might happen

i hung on
to the
penniless
parts of my existence
in love - in money - in friendships
in sickness
all for you
do you freaking hear that?
all for you, people
so that you will be moved
out of your own existential crisis
when you
hear about mine,
so you could shake your head
back and forth
and say,

"oh, poor penniless her,
my partner's better,
at least he text-ed.
poor her, i read her poem,
she rotted on a park bench
in the thunderstorm
and lightning
soaked to the bone
sobbing
and he still didn't say
i love you
back."

terrible news
i'm not sad anymore
do you know why
because i lost
the big
giant box of safety pins
that i used
to pin my life together
every night and day
when things fell apart
and what does one do
with no safety pins
to pin their world together?
one stands and watches
their own train wreck of a life
go off the rails
in high speed

terrible news
i'm not sad anymore
watching the train of life
one car at a time
tumble
off the rails
was/is strangely cathartic
surprise.
that's where the peace is
who knew

so i have peace and calm
and silence
no noise
no speed
no train tracks
no more sad poems
no fear
because it all already
happened

and i'm here
to tell you a secret
it's not that bad
sitting at the edge
that's where you find
what some people call
the essence
of
you,
nothingness
and
everything-ness.

not at the end
of the rainbow
but at the beginning
of
the dark night
where you say goodbye
to writing sad poems
i never knew sadness
has an end
but it does,
i tell you. it does.

so, follow me on the journey
up and down
the yellow brick road
to the awakened sun
leading to
the secret of the other side
of sadness
and train wrecks
where no safety pins
are needed ever again
because
do you know
where the path of destruction
leads?

Freedom.
it leads to Freedom.

if god read minds

if god reads minds
and i don't know
if he does
he would know my little secret
that i pray for your demise

oh, i nod at the right words,
like
'it happened for a reason,
you will grow and move along'
or 'lessons learned,
onto
something/someone better.'
but i do the thing that's wrong
putting everything aside
i pray for your demise.

if god reads minds
and i don't know if he does
he knows i'm nice
i want the best for all the rest
of beings in the world
well, except for
you.

my purple book of
psalms
is tear stained
and emotion drained
because
i know how to pray
when life calls out
for souls to come together
to weather
the storms of life
for each other
and pray
i do
but not for you
well not for you anymore

i leave thoughts of you
behind in the dust
the kind of dust
that comes out of the
tailpipe
of the past
gray and musty dusty
and forgotten

if god reads minds
and i don't know if he does
he would know i don't approve
of lessons learned this way
by meeting the wrong
then leaving the wrong
way too late
no hate
no shade
i'm just praying
in the wrong direction
just for a second

to set the record straight
for those that are too good
to tell god
what they really want to
happen
to those they now despise
but i don't hide, i say it
like it is
something like this,

'god, take a spoonful of that
medicine you give
from the jar
of lessons, the spoonful
with no sugar'

and when all settles down
and they have it made
heading to the sunset
mix a spoonful
of their past actions
into their morning cereal and
milk

if god reads minds
and i don't know if he does
he would look at me and nod
and say,

'you don't have to pray for
anyone's demise for they
wake up every day and lose a
little peace'

that's what's given back to me
a piece of peace from them
becomes
peace for me
and checks and balance
reigns supreme
for any being harmed
by another
it's the way of the world

not to worry about
praying someone down
to the ground
to the pain
they caused others
they'll have
their turn to
learn
their lessons

no one gets away
scot-free
fancy free
and gets to drive into the
sunset
while causing others pain

we just don't always get
to see this
played out
for real

but if we keep
our eyes
ahead
we know for sure
that with lessons learned
by being with the wrong
it takes us to the right
we end up in the light
shining bright

where all is right
with prayer
in
the world

Conclusion

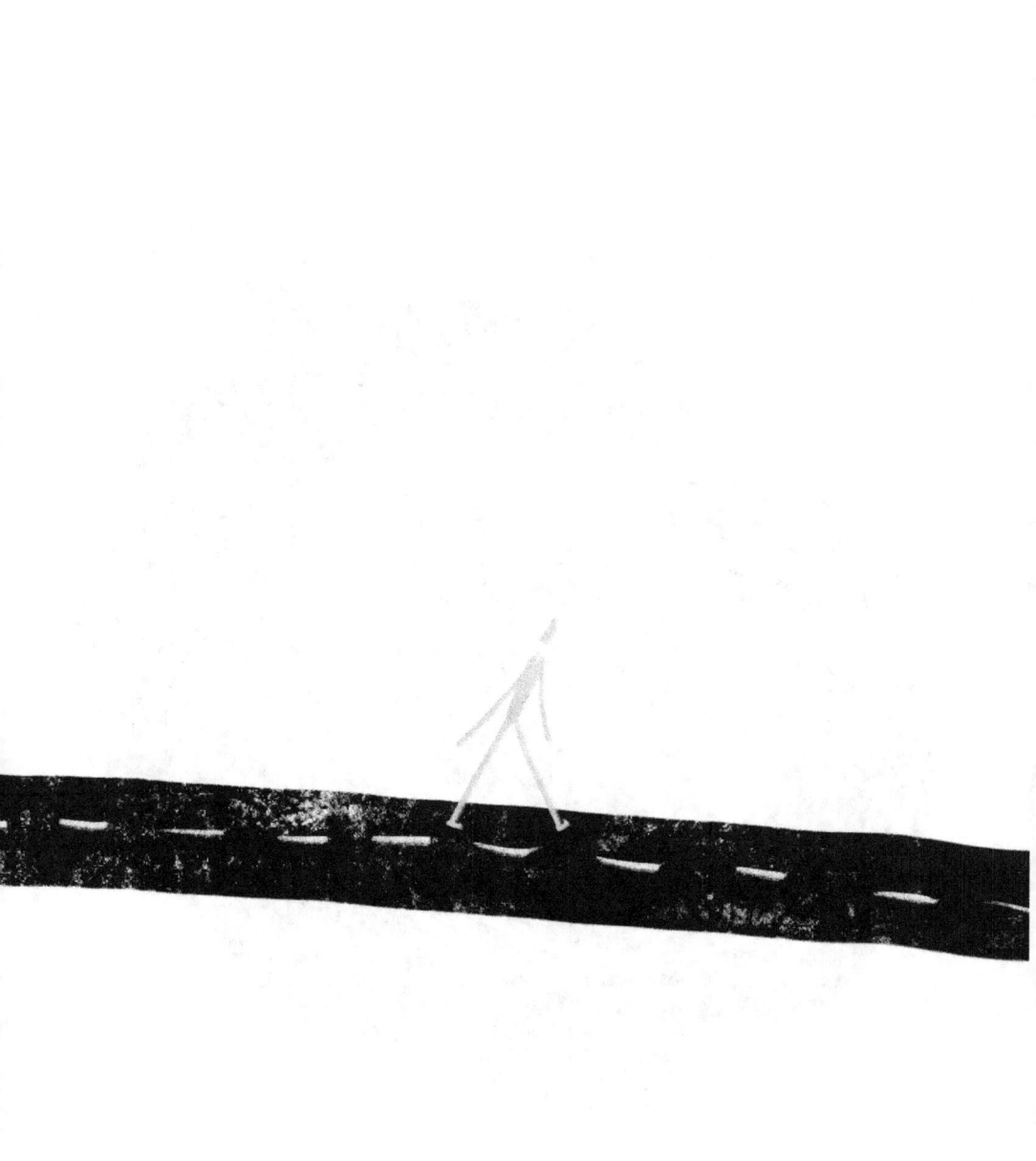

with apologies for sad poems

i apologize
for the sadness
between these poetry
pages
but it's been ages
since
i felt
otherwise.

i tell lies
day in and day out
to feign happiness
and hope
so those around me
that have their own
compass to follow
don't stall
and stumble
and fumble
over
my melodrama
and
broken direction.

not everyone
gets to ride
a stable ship
or luxury liner
down the coast of life
to Ibiza
some like me
get the five cent ferry
from Staten Island
to New York City

that rickety thing
gets you
across the waters of life
and into
a seemingly successful
city
where you're told
you could make it
with a prayer
and
the dollar in your pocket

but the truth is
that one is lucky
if they can grab a spot

to hang on to the handrail
so they don't
go overboard
unnoticed
never to be missed
by anyone

i apologize
for the sadness
between these poetry
pages
i was planning on making this
a happy and funny apology
at the end of my book
like
ha ha, all is good in the world,
i only drown my dark nights
of the soul
in my poems
once in a while
but my days are
bright and cheerful

i have books of poems
full of gratitude lists

and manifestations
and hidden boxes
of
golden coins
ha ha all is well

but it's not coming out
that way
my poems take on
a life of their own
i have no control
of the truth telling
of
these
little sonnets
they spill out sloppily
all over the place
without my permission

i apologize for
the sadness
between these poetry
pages
as i watch
from
the sidelines of life

i sit in a dark room
at 12:29 am
trying to
pump out
happy thoughts
but i'm so sorry
i don't have any.

i had some great thoughts
earlier
and yesterday
but they didn't last
too long
they come and go
those happy thoughts
while the
Staten Island ferry
rocks back and forth
not gently
i mean it's New York
nothing is gentle there
trust me i know
i was born and raised there,
a proud New Yorker
that could withstand
anything

having said that
i makes no apologies
for the sadness
between these poetry
pages
because
i mean tomorrow, tomorrow
i love you tomorrow
if i could make it here
i could make it anywhere
and i have all these grand
plans
i never gave up
on

like when i was a kid
and wanted to be a ballerina
i mean that could
still happen
i never dreamed of
being the best
and youngest ballerina
just a ballerina
because i loved to dance
and wanted a
pink
tutu

so i could still do that
and love it
and dance in the
mirror
and feel myself
move to the music
and watch myself spin

having said that
i make no apologies for
the sadness
between these poetry
pages i mean JK Rowling
was once sad too
i mean she wasn't
on a ferry
she was on a train
heading nowhere
like me
with a pen and a
dream

it came true for her
it could happen for me
we could be twins
two failures
on crappy transportation

that turned into
the writers
we dreamed of
wow i'm getting happier
already

having said that
i make no apologies for the
sadness
between these
poetry pages
i'm a future ballerina
and a writer
now that's me
achieving my dreams
what could possibly
be better than that

well if you come
along for the ride
and bring your dream on board
whatever your dream may be
with me and JK
i promise we'll ride
first class
cz thats what
dreams do

they take you from
darkness
and pain
and sad words
and horrid ferries and
trains
to lands
where you get to live
the life you imagine
we imagine
with wizards

and one by one
we take each other
along

and the world is
full of dreamers
and achievers
sad poems come
and sad poems go

forever

and

ever

Amen.

Contact:
ESTHERFINK.COM
201-378-3996
esther@estherfink.com